Vera Dale

A Holiday Adventure

Ernst Klett Stuttgart

Contents

1. Auflage 1[8] 7 6 | 1976 75 74

Alle Drucke dieser Auflage können im Unterricht nebeneinander benutzt werden. Die letzte Zahl bezeichnet das Jahr dieses Druckes.

Illustrationen: Walter Rieck, Heilbronn.
Druck: Ernst Klett, 7 Stuttgart, Rotebühlstraße 77.
Printed in Germany.
ISBN 3-12-531500-x

Mike Buys Presents

In June 1966, Mike and fourteen boys of his class were in Austria with their teacher, Mr Miller. They saw many lovely old towns and beautiful castles. They also visited factories with modern machines, and farms. They had taken lots of photographs of oxen, cows and calves with bells round their necks, of buildings, bridges, and churches, of high mountains and lovely rivers.

One day Mike met Tom at the door of their hotel in Innsbruck.

"Hallo, Mike, where are you going?" asked Tom.

"I must buy some souvenirs for my family," said Mike. "Come with me."

They went into a big shop. Mike bought a pair of gloves for his mother, a hairbrush and comb for his sister, a packet of cigarettes for his father and a teddy bear for his little brother.

"Don't you want to buy anything?" Mike asked his friend.

2–5315/1

"Yes," said Tom. "I want to buy some soap for my grandparents, and a ball-point pen for my cousin Betty, but I haven't enough money for that."

"How much money do you need?"

"I've got fifteen shillings, but I need twenty."

"Austrian or English shillings?"

"Austrian shillings, of course."

"All right," said Mike. "Carry my parcel and you can have the five shillings."

"All right," said Tom and took the parcel from Mike.

Then he bought the soap for his grandparents and the ball-point pen for his cousin, a manager's secretary in a big London office.

"Let's go to a café and have some coffee," said Mike as they came out into the street. Tom was carrying his parcel and Mike's parcel. In the café he put the two parcels under the table.

"They always bring a glass of water with the coffee," said Tom.

"It's a good idea," said Mike. "You can stay much longer. Look, all the people here are reading newspapers. There are English newspapers, too."

The waiter heard this and brought them two English newspapers.

"Here is good news for you," he said. "Look at the football reports. England won against Austria, but it was a good game."

Mike and Tom read and read and forgot the time. Suddenly Mike looked at his watch.

"It's late," he said. "We didn't think of the time. We must hurry back to the hotel. We mustn't make Mr Miller angry."

They paid for their coffee and left the café.

Suddenly Mike stopped. "Where are our parcels?" he asked.

Tom had a long face.

"I . . . I forgot them. They are under the table in the café," he said.

"Oh no!" shouted Mike. "And I gave you five shillings for that. You are the biggest ox in Austria and England together. We can say 'good-bye' to those parcels now."

"Perhaps they are still under the table," said Tom.

"Those parcels have got new friends, I tell you," said Mike.

"What's the matter?" asked Mr Miller as Mike and Tom entered the dining-room of the hotel with long faces. "You don't look very happy."

Mike told Mr Miller about the parcels.

"Go back to that café after lunch," said Mr Miller, "and ask the waiter."

They were sitting at a long dining-table. Their Austrian holiday was over. They had loved every moment of it and hated to leave that beautiful country.

"Oh, Mr Miller, why can't we stay any longer?" asked one of the boys.

“Don’t be funny,” answered Mr Miller. “You talk a lot of nonsense sometimes, Tim. Denis, please, must you make those noises with your spoon? The lady at the next table is getting impatient with you.”

“Mr Miller, why can’t we fly back? The plane is much quicker than the train,” asked another boy.

“But not so cheap,” was Mr Miller’s dry answer. “May I have the cheese, please?”

The waiter brought some fruit: cherries, peaches and pears.

“Don’t eat too much fruit, boys,” said Mr Miller. “It’s not good for your stomachs. I don’t want to take you to the doctor’s if you have stomach-aches. Now, listen! Our train leaves Innsbruck tonight at eight o’clock.”

After lunch Mike and Tom hurried back to the café.

“Yes,” said the waiter, “here are your parcels. I found them under the table.” He gave them to the boys.

This time Mike did not ask Tom to carry his parcel for five shillings.

Lost in Cologne

They arrived at Cologne at noon on June 14th, and went by bus to their hotel. The driver showed them some interesting old buildings and churches. The boys compared the road signs with those in England. Most of them were the same as in their country.

"We are spending the weekend in Cologne," said Mr Miller after lunch. "You may do what you like this afternoon. Go shopping and buy some food for the journey. Make a list first, write it in German."

"We don't know enough German for that," said one of the boys.

"That doesn't matter," answered Mr Miller. "At least you can practise it. Try to pronounce it well. Denis, your shirt is dirty, go and put on another shirt."

"All my shirts are dirty, Mr Miller. We couldn't do our washing in Austria."

"Well, put on a pullover, then, and your socks. Mike, you must clean your shoes before you go. Bob, go to the hairdresser's. Your hair is much too long."

"May we go to the zoo and feed the animals?" asked Tim.

"That's a good idea. You may also go for a walk in the park and feed the geese and ducks at the pond."

"What happens if we lose our way, Mr Miller?"

"The name of our hotel is the Royal. The telephone number is four–one–seven–double-six. Learn it by heart and write it on a piece of paper, for your memory is not too good. And take a map of Cologne with you."

Most of the boys went to see the town, but some felt so tired that they stayed in their rooms and lay on their beds during the afternoon. Mike and Tom went out together. First they went to the stationer's where they bought some writing-paper and picture postcards.

"I must write a line to my parents," said Mike.

"I've written to all my relations," said Tom. "I forgot nobody, I think."

At the baker's they bought a loaf of bread and a dozen rolls, at the butcher's some sausages.

"We still need a pound of tomatoes and a tin of pineapple," said Tom as they left the butcher's.

"Most of the people here speak English," said Mike. "Did you hear how that shop-assistant said 'do you want anything else'?"

"Let's go to a cinema now," said Tom. "I want to see a funny film. Look, there is one round the corner."

When they came out of the cinema, they did not know the way back to the hotel.

"Let's ask the way," said Mike.

"In English or German?" asked Tom.

"In German, of course," said Mike.

He went straight to a man with a green scarf round his neck.

"Entschuldige mich, kannst du zeigen mir den Weg zum Royal Hotel?"

The man looked at him, but did not answer.

"Try it in English," said Tom. "He doesn't understand. Your German is not good enough."

"Excuse me," repeated Mike in English. "Can you show me the way to the Royal Hotel?"

The man looked at him again and said: "Nix versteh. Italiano."

"He comes from Italy," said Mike. "He's an Italian. That's why he couldn't understand my German."

They studied the map of Cologne, turned right, turned left, and walked through wide and narrow streets. A quarter of an hour later they saw the cinema again.

"It's no use," said Mike. "We must ask the way again."

"It's my turn to ask," said Tom and spoke to a woman in a red skirt and black stockings.

"Entschuldige mich, kannst du zeigen mir den Weg zum Royal Hotel?"

"Nix versteh. Española," said the woman.

"She is Spanish and comes from Spain," said Tom. "They must have a lot of visitors here."

"Are there any Germans in this town?" asked Mike. "Let's ask that boy with the bike."

They asked the boy in German, but he answered in English.

"You must take a bus. The bus stop is just at the corner. Take a number 36 bus and get out at the third stop. Do you come from England?"

"Yes," said Tom. "From London."

"I was in London last month with my class," said the boy. "That's a very big city. I couldn't find my way through the streets."

"What did you do?"

"Same as you. I asked. Look, there is your bus. Bye-bye."

"At last!" said Mr Miller as Mike and Tom arrived at the Royal. "Better late than never, but better never late."

A Friendly Stranger

Two days later Mike and the other boys of his class were waiting at Cologne Station for the train to Ostend. Mr Miller had gone to buy a newspaper for the journey. Mike was standing a few steps away from the others. Suddenly somebody behind him spoke to him. Mike turned round and saw a tall man.

"On your way to London, son?" asked the man.

"Yes," said Mike. "We've been on holiday in Austria."

"Perhaps you can help me," said the man and looked at Mike with a smile. He took a small packet out of his trousers' pocket. "This must reach London tomorrow. It's my brother's medicine. He must take it every day, but he left Cologne this morning without his medicine. I found it in the cupboard of my living-room after he had gone. My poor brother is in great danger if he doesn't get his medicine. It's all very sad."

"I don't know your brother," said Mike.

"That doesn't matter," said the man. "I can telephone him and tell him that you have his medicine. Look for a tall man

in a brown suit with a hanky in his left hand. Give him the packet when you see him at Victoria Station in London. Can you do that for me?"

The man took two bank-notes out of his pocket.

"Oh, ten pounds!" said Mike.

"It's a little present for you. Thank you very much. You're really very kind. Good-bye."

The man gave Mike the packet and the money, turned round and hurried away.

Mike went back to his friends. At that moment Mr Miller came back. "Are you ready, boys?" he asked. "Carry your bags to the train."

The Mysterious Packet

In the train Mike told his friends about the man, the packet and the money.

"Aren't you lucky!" said Tim.

"Tell Mr Miller," said Bob. "He likes to hear a good story." Mike went to his teacher.

"I hope I'm not disturbing you, Mr Miller, but I must tell you something."

After Mike's story Mr Miller became very serious. "I wonder if it is a medicine at all," he said. "The packet may be in order, of course. But you never know. Perhaps those people are smugglers."

The boys looked at their teacher.

"But the gentleman was so kind and polite," said Mike who was very disappointed. "He offered me ten pounds and I took them."

"That's just it," said Mr Miller. "Ten pounds is much too much money for what you have to do. We must be prepared for everything."

"What can we do?" asked Mike. "Let's open the packet and see what is in it. I have a pair of scissors in my bag."

"No, no," said Mr Miller. "I have an idea. Do what the man said."

The train was racing through Belgium. Suddenly a Belgian policeman came to them. He was looking for Mr Miller. Mike's face felt as hot as fire. What did the policeman want? 'This is awful,' he thought. 'It's my fault. Why did I take the packet from that man? The police are looking for me!'

"Are these your boys?" said the policeman to Mr Miller.

"Yes, they are."

"Tell them not to throw bottles out of the windows," said the policeman. "They could hurt somebody. We don't want an accident. That mustn't happen again."

Dangerous Medicine

On the boat from Ostend to Dover Mr Miller telephoned to Scotland Yard in London and told the police about the packet with the medicine.

During the crossing it was windy and as they reached Dover it began to rain.

"The weather is worse here than in Austria," said Denis.

They got wet and cold on the way from the boat to the train. On the train to London Mr Miller called the boys together and said:

"Now comes the big test. Here are my orders: don't get excited and remember the Boy Scouts' motto 'be prepared'. I want to be proud of you."

Two hours later the train arrived at Victoria Station. All the boys were looking out of the windows.

"There he is, Mike," said Mr Miller and he looked at a tall man in a brown suit. The man was holding a hanky in his left hand.

"This is the worst part," thought Mike as he got out of the train. He went straight to the man.

"This is from your brother in Cologne," he said and gave him the packet.

At that moment two policemen came and stood behind the man. "Excuse me," said one of them. "May I see that packet?"

The man turned round as quick as lightning and tried to run away, but the policeman caught him. The packet fell to the ground. Mike picked it up and gave it to one of the policemen who opened it. It was full of diamonds.

"This man is under arrest," said one policeman. Mike took the ten pounds out of his pocket.

"The man in Cologne gave them to me," said Mike.

"They are for you," said the policeman with the diamonds. "You've helped us to catch Robby Longfingers. He is a very dangerous thief."

Robby Longfingers was soon in the police car and they drove him to Scotland Yard.

A reporter was among the people at the station. "Just a moment, please," he said to Mike. "Can you give me an interview?"

"Well," Mike began. "It was really simple enough. A gangster at Cologne Station gave me a packet for his brother in London. 'It's medicine' he said."

"How did you know that the man in Cologne was a gangster?" asked the reporter.

"Oh, I guessed that because he gave me such a lot of money."

And the reporter wrote a report.

'British Boy Catches Dangerous Gangster' was in all the newspapers next day, also a big picture of Mike.

Exercises

Mike Buys Presents

1. Mike's photographs. On Mike's photographs we could see

a) Mike took photographs of ...
b) In Austria there are old ... and modern ...
... high ... and low ... — ... big ... and small ...

2. One—two. *Read and write:* A ... — two ...

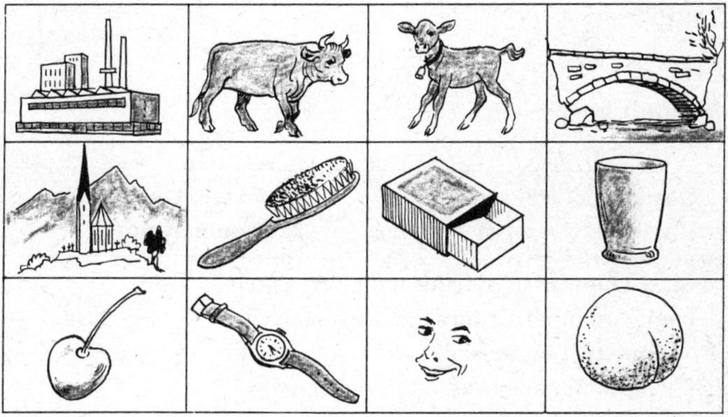

3. Don't forget

a cup **of** tea	a pair **of** gloves
a cup **of** coffee	a packet **of** cigarettes
a glass **of** water	a piece **of** cake
a loaf **of** bread	a box **of** soap

4. Mike's and Tom's souvenirs

Mike and Tom wanted to buy

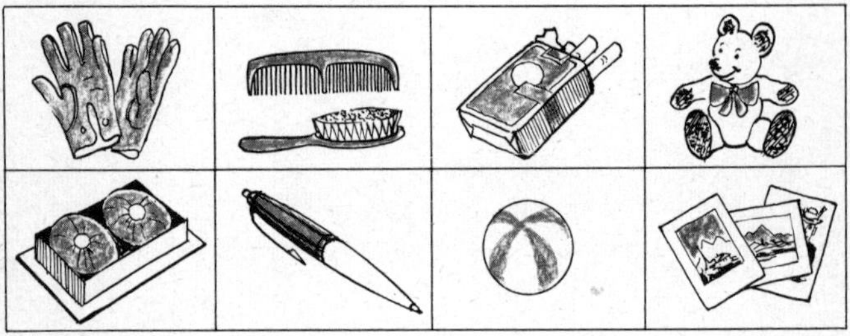

They bought a . . . for . . .

5. Don't forget

May I drink a glass of water? — Of course, **you may.** **May we** buy a lot of souvenirs? — No, **you may not.**
Mike, **you mustn't drink** too much water. Tom, **you mustn't buy** too many souvenirs. We **mustn't come** back late. The boys **mustn't make** too much noise.

6. In the dining-room. The waiter brought a ... (some ...)

a) *The boys asked their teacher:* "May I have a ... (some ...)?
What did the teacher answer?

b) The waiter gave Tom (Mike, Peter, Bob ...) a ... (some ...)?

c) *The teacher said:* "You mustn't eat (drink) too much ..."

7. Did you read well? *Then fill in what they did.*

The English boys ... many interesting things in Austria.
They ... lots of photographs.
One day Mike ... Tom at the door of their hotel.
They ... to buy some souvenirs for their ...
They ... to a big shop.
Tom ... twenty shillings for his presents.
He ... Mike's parcels.
Mike ... him five shillings for that.
They ... to a café.
Tom ... the parcels under the table.
The waiter ... them two ... coffee and an English ...
They ... at the football ...
England ... against Austria.
The boys ... and ...
They ... the time.
They ... for their coffee and ... the café.

Lost in Cologne

1. Let's compare some road signs

German road signs

English road signs

2. Have you a good memory? *Then put the right words together.*

a picture postcard	of bread
a map	of tomatoes
a pound	of the pond
a piece	of the hotel
the telephone number	of the big bridge
the animals	of paper
the geese	of the bus
the driver	of the zoo
a loaf	of pineapple
a tin	of Cologne

3. Don't forget

Give **me** some milk.	This milk is for **me.**
May I give **you** some milk?	This milk is for **you.**
Give **him** some milk.	This milk is for **him.**
Give **her** some milk.	This milk is for **her.**
Give **it** some milk.	This milk is for **it.**
Give **us** some milk.	This milk is for **us.**
Give **them** some milk.	This milk is for **them.**

4. The shops

At the baker's	a pencil	some rolls
At the butcher's	a book	some sausage
At the stationer's	a ball-point pen	some writing-paper
At the grocer's	a pullover	some tomatoes
In the book shop	a comb	a loaf of bread
In the big shop	a shirt	a tin of milk
	a note-book	a map of the town
	picture postcards	a piece of cake
	socks	a pound of sugar
	a dozen eggs	a box of soap

a) Mike goes shopping.
At the baker's he buys ...
At the butcher's ... *and so on.*

b) If we need a ... (some ...) we must go to ...

c) *I say to the shop-assistant:*
"I want a ... (some ...)."
"Please, give me ..."

d) I want a ... some ... The shop-assistant gives me ...
Go on: you, Peter, Betty, we, the boys.

5. Lost in the town

a) We couldn't find . . .
b) *We asked somebody:* "Please, can you show us the way to . . .?"
c) *Mike asked:* "Excuse me, is there . . . in this street?"
d) It's my turn to ask the way to . . .
e) Nobody could show us the way to . . .

6. Did you read well? *Then fill in.*

Most of the boys . . . very tired and . . . in their rooms.
Some boys . . . out and . . . the town.
They . . . the telephone number of the hotel on a piece of paper.
Some of them . . . it by heart.
Bob . . . to the hairdresser's because his hair . . . very long.
Tim . . . to the park and . . . the geese and the ducks.
Mike and Tom . . . some writing-paper.
Mike . . . some postcards to his relations.
He . . . nobody.
They . . . to a cinema.
When they . . . out of the cinema they . . . their way back to the hotel.
At last they . . . a number 36 bus.

A Friendly Stranger

1. Our clothes

Boys wear

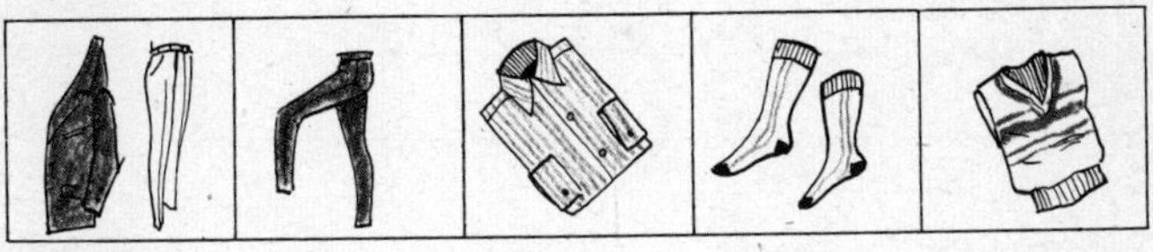

Girls wear

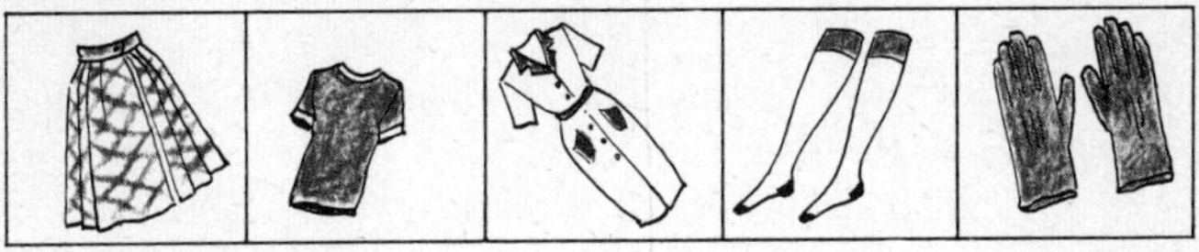

Everybody has a  in his pocket.

In winter we put a  round our necks.

a) *What colour are your clothes?*

b) *Answer.*

Which is warmer—a shirt or a pullover?
Which is longer—a stocking or a sock?
Which do girls wear—skirts or shirts?
Which are cheaper—shoes or hankies?
Which is better in winter—big pockets or a pair of gloves?

2. Don't forget

the boy**s**' teacher the girl**s**' hankies their parent**s**' money the Miller**s**' car	the children'**s** father the men'**s** trousers the women'**s** bags the policemen'**s** cars
s'	**'s**

3. Form new sentences

Example: This boy's present is nice.
These boys' presents are nice. *Go on.*

1. This baker's cake is good. 2. This butcher's sausage is big. 3. This child's brother is tall. 4. That teacher's pupil is all right. 5. That policeman's car is dirty. 6. This man's trousers are brown. 7. That girl's bike is red. 8. This child's room is small. 9. This shop-assistant's job is interesting. 10. That man's child is ill.

4. Let's help the police. They are looking for two strangers: an Austrian man and an Italian lady.

He is about 40 years old.	She is younger.
He is tall.	She is small.
He is thin.	She is fat.
He has fair hair.	She has dark hair.
He has short hair.	She has long hair.
He has blue eyes.	She has brown eyes.
He has a long neck.	She has a short neck.
He speaks English.	She doesn't speak English.
He wears brown trousers and a white shirt.	She wears a black skirt and a red pullover.

a) *Yesterday Mike saw such a man in the underground. He telephoned the police. What did he tell them?*

b) *Tom was sitting near a lady in the bus who looked like the Italian lady. What did he tell the police?*

c) *What can you tell about the boy or the girl who is sitting near you?*

5. The stranger

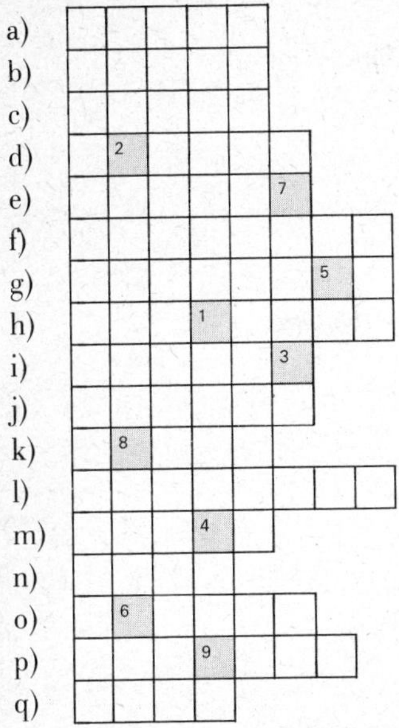

a) Mike was standing a few ... away from the others.
b) Suddenly a man ... to him.
c) He looked at Mike with a ...
d) He gave him a ...
e) He took it out of his ...
f) He took it out of a pocket of his ...
g) There was his brothers ... in the packet.
h) He had found it in a ...
i) That morning his brother had taken the train to ...
j) He was in ... without his medicine.
k) It had to ... him the next day.
l) His brother was waiting at ... station.
m) He had a ... in his left hand.
n) Mike ... the parcel.
o) The man gave him ten ...
p) That was a ... for Mike.
q) Mike was very ...

In the boxes with numbers you can see what else the man had in his pocket.

6. From the Cologne hotel to the station

We ... our bag.	*Use:* to get out
We ... the hotel.	to go
We ... to the bus stop.	to leave
We ... for the bus.	to look
We ... in the bus.	to sit down
We ... at the station.	to take
We ... for our train.	to wait

Tell it once more. What did the English boys do?

The Mysterious Packet

1. Mr Miller became serious. *He thought:*

What is in the packet?
Is it medicine at all?
Is the packet really for his brother?
Is his brother really in danger?
Is the stranger a smuggler?

He said: I wonder what is in ...?
I wonder if it is ...?—*Go on.*

2. Do you remember what they were like?

The packet was ...
Tim said to Mike: "Aren't you ...!"
After Mike's story his teacher became ...
The stranger was ... and ...—Mike was very ...
In the train Mike's face felt as ... as fire.

3. Something is wrong here. *Find it out.*

Mike bought

a bottle	of tomatoes
a packet	of pineapple
a pound	of milk
a piece	of gloves
a pair	of bread
a cup	of envelopes
a loaf	of cake
a tin	of coffee

4. Some countries round Germany

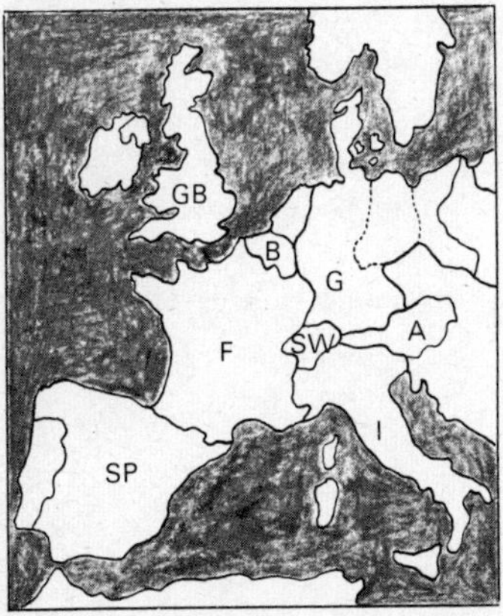

Are you clever? Then answer.

Where is London?
Where is Cologne?
Where is Innsbruck?
Where is Ostend?
Where is Paris?
In what countries are there high mountains?
What do they speak in Spain?

What is wrong here?

In England	they speak French.
In Germany	they speak Italian.
In Italy	they speak Spanish.
In Spain	they speak German, French and Italian.
In Switzerland	they speak German.

Dangerous Medicine

1. Learn again and don't forget

What do you want?	Was wünschen Sie?
Do you want anything else?	Wünschen Sie sonst noch etwas?
Just a moment, please.	Einen Augenblick, bitte.
It's my turn.	Ich bin an der Reihe.
Let's have a coffee.	Wir wollen einen Kaffee trinken.
I lost my way.	Ich habe mich verirrt.
I asked the way.	Ich fragte nach dem Weg.
Excuse me, can you tell me the way to ...?	Entschuldigen Sie bitte, können Sie mir den Weg nach... zeigen?
Take a number 36 bus.	Fahren Sie mit einem Bus der Linie 36.
Walk round the next corner.	Gehen Sie um die nächste Ecke.
Say it in English, please.	Sagen Sie es bitte auf Englisch.
My English isn't good enough.	Ich spreche nicht gut genug englisch.
I hope I'm not disturbing you?	Hoffentlich störe ich Sie nicht?
What's the matter?	Was ist los?
Don't be funny!	Sei nicht albern!
Don't talk nonsense.	Rede keinen Unsinn.
I'm getting impatient with you.	Du regst mich auf.
That mustn't happen again.	Das darf nicht wieder vorkommen.
It's my fault.	Es ist meine Schuld.
That doesn't matter.	Das macht nichts.
My face felt as hot as fire.	Ich wurde feuerrot im Gesicht.
We couldn't do our washing.	Wir konnten unsere Wäsche nicht waschen.

We couldn't stay any longer.	Wir konnten nicht länger bleiben.
Write the telephone number on a piece of paper.	Schreiben Sie die Telefonnummer auf ein Stück Papier.
You never know.	Man kann nie wissen.
Learn it by heart.	Lernen Sie sie auswendig.
My memory is very good.	Ich habe ein sehr gutes Gedächtnis.
It was no use.	Es war umsonst.
I must write a line to my parents.	Ich muß meinen Eltern ein paar Zeilen schreiben.
The smuggler turned round as quick as lightning.	Der Schmuggler drehte sich blitzschnell um.
The policeman said: "You're under arrest."	Der Polizist sagte: „Sie sind verhaftet".

3. Put together the right words

a)

dry	old
better	slow
young	awful
quick	small
wonderful	later
hot	fat
tall	wet
earlier	different
thin	worse
happy	cold
same	dirty
clean	long
short	narrow
wide	sad

b)

to arrive	to sell
to find	to come
to remember	to leave
to go	to lose
to buy	to forget

c)

in front of	after
always	nobody
everything	never
first	behind
somebody	nothing
before	at last

d)

question	gangster
policeman	pupil
teacher	answer

2. Can you say another word for

the London Police Station?
the journey from Ostend to Dover?
to leave the train?
very quick?
to take something from the ground?
a man who takes away other people's things?
to tell a reporter what had happened?
what the reporters write in the newspaper?

4. From one place to another. *This is what we can take:*

What do you take? You want to go

from Innsbruck to Cologne.
from Ostend to Dover.
from Cologne to America.
from Victoria Station to Scotland Yard.
from Cologne Station to your hotel.

Say it once more. I go from ... to ... by ...

Answer.

Which is quicker—the train or the plane?
Which is cheaper—the boat or the plane?
Which is heavier—a bus or a plane?
Which is longer—a train or an underground train?

5. Verb Test. *Fill in.*

Today	*Yesterday*
....	he went
I bring	....
....	they won
you carry	....
they buy	....
....	he got
I write	....
....	we lay
....	they felt
....	they fell
....	she lost
we give	....
....	you left
they find	....
we come	....
I drive	....
he stands	....

....	it took
....	she met
....	he put
I hear	....
you learn	....
....	they read
....	we told
he holds	....
they begin	....
....	he caught
she thinks	....
....	we spoke
we see	....
you are	....
they make	....
....	she paid

6. Big test. *Did you read the story well?*

Where did the boys spend their holidays?
Where is Innsbruck?
What do they speak in Austria?

What did they visit in Austria?
What do the cows and the calves wear round their necks in Austria and Switzerland?
What money do you need in Austria?
Are there shillings in England, too?
Where is Tom's cousin working?
What do the Austrian waiters bring with the coffee?
Can you buy English and German newspapers in Austria?
What's the name of the room in a hotel where people have their lunch and their breakfast?
What happens if you eat too much fruit?
At what time is noon?
Where is Cologne?
Are there any bridges in Cologne?
Why were the boys' clothes all dirty?
Where must you go if your hair is too long?
Where must you go if you want to see a lot of different animals?
What animals can you feed at a pond?
What do you do if you can't find your way?
Where do you buy writing-paper?
What can you buy at the baker's?
Where must you go if you need a pound of sugar?
Why do you go to the cinema?
What countries do you know?
What do people speak in these countries?
Is there an underground in Cologne?
Where do you go if you feel ill?
What do you take to get better?
At what London station do the trains from Dover arrive?
What's the name of a man who takes diamonds from one country to another?
Are smugglers thieves? Are they gangsters?
What's the name of the people who write for newspapers?

Word List

Mike Buys Presents

Austria [ˈɔstriə]	Österreich
lovely [ˈlʌvli]	hübsch, schön
castle [ˈkɑ:sl]	Schloß, Burg
also [ˈɔ:lsou]	ebenfalls, auch
factory [ˈfæktəri] **(*Mz.* -ies)**	Fabrik
modern [ˈmɔdən]	modern
machine [məˈʃi:n]	Maschine
taken [ˈteikən] **(to take)**	*hier:* gemacht
ox (*Mz.* oxen) [ɔks, ˈɔksən]	Ochse
calf (*Mz.* calves) [kɑ:f, kɑ:vz]	Kalb
building [ˈbildiŋ]	Gebäude
bridge [bridʒ]	Brücke
church [tʃə:tʃ] **(*Mz.* -es)**	Kirche
high [hai]	hoch
mountain [ˈmauntin]	Berg
river [ˈrivə]	Fluß
I met [met] **(to meet)**	ich traf
hotel [houˈtel]	Hotel
souvenir [ˈsu:vəniə]	Andenken
big shop	*hier:* Kaufhaus
I bought [bɔ:t] **(to buy)**	ich kaufte
pair [pɛə]	Paar
gloves [glʌvz]	Handschuhe
hairbrush [ˈhɛəbrʌʃ] **(*Mz.* -es)**	Haarbürste
comb [koum]	Kamm
packet [ˈpækit]	Packung, Päckchen

cigarette [sigəˈret]	Zigarette
teddy bear [ˈtediˌbɛə]	Plüschbär
soap [soup]	Seife
grandparents [ˈgrænpɛərənts]	Großeltern
ball-point pen [ˈbɔ:lpɔint ˈpen]	Kugelschreiber
cousin [ˈkʌzn]	Vetter, Base
I've got [gɔt]	ich habe
shilling [ˈʃiliŋ]	1. engl. Münze (etwa 55 Pf) 2. österreichische Münze (etwa 16 Pf)
Austrian [ˈɔstriən]	österreichisch
to carry [ˈkæri]	tragen
parcel [ˈpɑ:sl]	Paket
manager [ˈmænidʒə]	Direktor
secretary [ˈsekrətri] **(*Mz.* -ies)**	Sekretärin
an office [ˈɔfis]	ein Büro
a London [ˈlʌndən] **office**	ein Londoner Büro
café [ˈkæfei]	Café
to have some coffee [ˈkɔfi]	(eine Tasse) Kaffee trinken
as [æz, əz]	als
I put [put] **(to put)**	ich setzte, stellte, legte
an idea [aiˈdiə]	eine Idee, ein Einfall
waiter [ˈweitə]	Kellner
I heard [hə:d] **(to hear)**	ich hörte

news [nju:z]	Neuigkeit
report [riˈpɔ:t]	Bericht
to win, won, won [win, wʌn]	gewinnen
against [əˈgenst]	gegen *(jdn)*
I read [red] **(to read)**	ich las
I forgot [fəˈgɔt] **(to forget)**	ich vergaß
to hurry back to [ˈhʌri]	schnell zurückgehen zu
I paid [peid] **(to pay)**	ich bezahlte
I left [left] **(to leave)**	ich verließ
to stop, stopped, stopped [stɔp, stɔpt]	stehenbleiben
I tell you	sage ich dir; glaube mir
to enter a room [ˈentə]	in einen Raum hineingehen, -kommen
dining-room [ˈdainiŋrum]	Eßzimmer; Speisesaal
dining-table [ˈdainiŋteibl]	Eßtisch
over [ˈouvə]	vorbei, vorüber
to love [lʌv]	lieben, gern haben, mögen
loved [lʌvd]	geliebt
moment [ˈmoumənt]	Augenblick
to hate [heit]	hassen, nicht mögen
can't we stay any longer? [ˈlɔŋgə]	können wir nicht länger (hier) bleiben?
funny [ˈfʌni]	spaßig, ulkig
don't be funny	sei nicht albern
nonsense [ˈnɔnsəns]	Unsinn
to talk [tɔ:k] **nonsense**	Unsinn reden
noise [nɔiz]	Geräusch, Lärm
spoon [spu:n]	Löffel
to get impatient [imˈpeiʃənt] **(got, got)**	ungeduldig werden
to get impatient with somebody	sich über jdn. aufregen
to fly, flew, flown [flai, flu:, floun]	fliegen
plane [plein] = **aeroplane** [ˈɛərəplein]	Flugzeug
cheap [tʃi:p]	billig
dry [drai]	trocken
cheese [tʃi:z]	Käse
cherry [ˈtʃeri] **(*Mz.* -ies)**	Kirsche
peach [pi:tʃ] **(*Mz.* peaches)**	Pfirsich
pear [pɛə]	Birne
stomach [ˈstʌmək]	Magen
to take somebody to the doctor's [ˈdɔktəz]	jdn. zum Arzt bringen
to have stomach-ache [ˈstʌməkeik]	Leibschmerzen haben
tonight [təˈnait]	heute abend

Lost in Cologne

lost [lɔst] **(to lose)**	verloren
Cologne [kəˈloun]	Köln
at noon [nu:n]	mittags, am Mittag
by bus [bʌs]	mit dem Bus
driver [ˈdraivə]	Fahrer
to compare with [kəmˈpɛə]	vergleichen mit

road sign [ˈroudsain]	Verkehrsschild
most of them [moust]	die meisten von ihnen
the same as [seim]	der-, die- dasselbe wie, genauso wie
to spend [spend], **spent, spent** [spent]	verbringen
weekend [ˈwi:kˈend]	Wochenende
journey [ˈdʒə:ni]	Reise
list [list]	Liste
first [fə:st]	zuerst
that doesn't matter [ˈmætə]	das macht nichts
at least [li:st]	wenigstens
to practise [ˈpræktis]	üben
to pronounce [prəˈnauns]	aussprechen
shirt [ˈʃə:t]	Hemd
I do my washing [ˈwɔʃiŋ]	ich wasche meine Wäsche
pullover [ˈpulouvə]	Pullover
socks [sɔks]	Socken
to clean [kli:n]	säubern, putzen
hairdresser [ˈhɛədresə]	Friseur
to go to the hairdresser's	zum Friseur gehen
to feed [fi:d], **fed, fed** [fed]	füttern
park [pɑ:k]	Park
goose [gu:s] **(*Mz.* geese)** [gi:s]	Gans
duck [dʌk]	Ente
pond [pɔnd]	Teich
I lose my way [lu:z] **(lost, lost)**	ich verlaufe mich
Royal Hotel [ˈrɔiəl]	*Hotelname*
double [ˈdʌbl]	doppel
double-six	sechs-sechs
heart [hɑ:t]	Herz
to learn [lə:n], **learnt,** [lə:nt] **learnt**	lernen
to learn by heart	auswendig lernen
for [fɔ:]	denn
memory [ˈmeməri] **(*Mz.* -ies)**	Gedächtnis
I lay (to lie) [lei]	ich legte mich
stationer [ˈsteiʃnə]	Schreibwarenhändler
to go to the stationer's	in ein Schreibwarengeschäft gehen
writing-paper [ˈraitiŋ peipə]	Briefpapier
postcard [ˈpoustkɑ:d]	Postkarte
picture postcard [ˈpiktʃə]	Ansichtskarte
to write, wrote, written [rait, rout, ˈritn]	schreiben
line [lain]	Linie, Zeile
to write a line	ein Paar Zeilen schreiben
the relations [riˈleiʃəns]	die Verwandten
nobody [ˈnoubədi]	niemand
baker [ˈbeikə]	Bäcker
at the baker's	beim Bäcker, in der Bäckerei
a loaf of bread [ˈlouf əv ˈbred]	ein Laib Brot
dozen [ˈdʌzn]	Dutzend
roll [roul]	Brötchen

butcher [ˈbutʃə]	Fleischer, Metzger
at the butcher's	beim Fleischer
sausage [ˈsɔsidʒ]	Wurst
pound [paund]	Pfund *(Gewicht, etwa 453 g)*
tomato [təˈmɑ:tou] (*Mz.* **tomatoes)**	Tomate
tin [tin]	Konservendose
pineapple [ˈpainæpl]	Ananas
shop-assistant [əˈsistənt]	Verkäufer, Verkäuferin
do you want anything else? [ˈeniθiŋ els]	darf es sonst noch etwas sein?
cinema [ˈsinəmə]	Kino
film [film]	Film
round the corner [ˈkɔ:nə]	um die Ecke
to ask the way [wei]	nach dem Weg fragen
scarf [skɑ:f]	Schal
to repeat [riˈpi:t]	wiederholen
Italiano [itʌlˈjɑ:no]	Italiener *(ital.)*
Italy [ˈitəli]	Italien
an Italian [iˈtæljən]	ein Italiener, eine Italienerin
that's why [wai]	deshalb
to study [ˈstʌdi]	studieren
wide [waid]	breit
narrow [ˈnærou]	eng
it's no use [ju:s]	es nützt nichts, es ist vergeblich
it's my turn [tə:n]	ich bin an der Reihe, ich bin dran
I spoke to [spouk] **(to speak)**	ich sprach mit
skirt [skə:t]	Rock *(f. Damen)*
stockings [ˈstɔkiŋz]	Damenstrümpfe
Española [espʌnˈjoulɑ:]	Spanierin *(spanisch)*
Spanish [ˈspæniʃ]	spanisch
she is Spanish	sie ist Spanierin
Spain [spein]	Spanien
visitor [ˈvizitə]	Besucher
bike [baik] = **bicycle**	Rad
bus stop [ˈbʌs ˈstɔp]	Bushaltestelle
a number 36 bus	ein Bus der Linie 36
to get out of [ˈget‿aut‿əv] **(got, got)**	aussteigen aus
city [ˈsiti] (*Mz.* **-ies)**	Großstadt
same as you [seim]	dasselbe wie ihr
bye-bye [ˈbai ˈbai] = **good-bye**	auf Wiedersehen
at last [lɑ:st]	endlich, schließlich

A Friendly Stranger

friendly [ˈfrendli]	freundlich
stranger [ˈstreindʒə]	Fremder, Fremde, Ausländer
station [ˈsteiʃən]	Bahnhof
Cologne Station [kəˈloun]	Kölner Bahnhof
Ostend [ɔsˈtend]	*Hafenstadt in Belgien*

I had gone [gɔn]	ich war gegangen
a few [fju:]	ein paar, einige
step [step]	Schritt
On your way to London, son?	Fährst du nach London, mein Junge?
I've been [bi:n] **on holiday**	ich bin in Ferien gewesen
smile [smail]	Lächeln
trousers [ˈtrauzəz]	(lange) Hose
trousers' pocket [ˈpɔkit]	Hosentasche
to reach [ri:tʃ]	erreichen, ankommen in
medicine [ˈmedsin]	Medizin, Arznei
cupboard [ˈkʌbəd]	Schrank
living-room [ˈliviŋrum]	Wohnzimmer
after he had gone [gɔn]	nachdem er gegangen war
danger [ˈdeindʒə]	Gefahr
sad [sæd]	traurig
suit [sju:t]	Herrenanzug
hanky [ˈhæŋki] **(*Mz.* -ies)**	Taschentuch
Victoria [vikˈtɔ:riə] **Station**	*ein Londoner Bahnhof*
bank-note [ˈbæŋknout]	Banknote, Geldschein
pound [paund]	*engl. Währungseinheit, etwa 11,20 DM*
really [ˈriəli]	wirklich
kind [kaind]	freundlich, nett
at that moment [ˈmoumənt]	in dem Augenblick, da
ready [ˈredi]	fertig

The Mysterious Packet

mysterious [misˈtiəriəs]	geheimnisvoll
aren't you lucky! [ˈlʌki]	was du für ein Glück hast!
to disturb [disˈtə:b]	stören
I hope I'm not disturbing you	hoffentlich störe ich Sie nicht
to become [biˈkʌm], **became** [biˈkeim], **become**	werden
serious [ˈsiəriəs]	ernst
I wonder if [ˈwʌndə]	ich möchte gern wissen, ob …
in order [ˈɔ:də]	in Ordnung
it may be in order	es mag, kann in Ordnung sein
you never know	man kann nie wissen
smuggler [ˈsmʌglə]	Schmuggler
gentleman [ˈdʒentlmən] **(*Mz.* -men)**	Herr
polite [pəˈlait]	höflich
who [hu:]	welcher, welche, welches; der, die, das
disappointed [disəˈpɔintid]	enttäuscht
to offer [ˈɔfə]	anbieten
to be prepared [priˈpɛəd] **for**	vorbereitet sein auf
everything [ˈevriθiŋ]	alles
(a pair of) scissors [ˈsizəz]	(eine) Schere
to race [reis]	rennen, sausen
Belgium [ˈbeldʒəm]	Belgien